WHO FARTED?

Quentin Hornblower

Plexus, London

T-Bone encouraged his master's relaxation
exercises but wished he'd lay off the pulses.

Takeaway night sometimes ended
badly for Charles and Prunella.

Karl grabbed the cat praying his allergies would kick in before Dita fragranced the room.

Clarence questioned if dogs, specifically Luther, were really man's best friend?

Monty usually employed the slow release technique like a pro, but something had malfunctioned. However, Samantha liked a man on the edge of control.

Tarquin was beginning to question the
safety of Lilly's laxative addiction.

Ludwig clenched with every ounce of his being to prevent his lunchtime fiber shake from ruining the ambassador's reception.

Howard wondered if this agony would ever end.

'Tell me you ate something other than chili-bean tacos this week?' Antonio may have taken his role as Zorro too far.

Verushka knew her father meant well but he was like
a one-man jazz band and things were getting 'Misty'.

'If we leave now, darling, it will take them weeks to work out who left this stain on the couch,' muttered Stanley.

Pervis wondered if looks actually could kill,
having just ingested one of Arthur's
scented after dinner mints.

Belinda knew the umbrella could not save her from Tibbins' stinging waft. Hugo, blissfully oblivious, lost his sense of smell years ago.

Carter thought his hat would protect him
from the acid rainmaker Wendy had just released.
He now had the suspicion it would be an exercise in futility.

Colonel Himlick slyly laid a methane bomb he knew would linger. Jaques had never hated him more.

'That's right – just pretend you're asleep, honey,'
thought Smythe. 'I know what you did.'

'Float like an air biscuit, stink like a bishop.'

Detective Carson now realised why they called her Cincinnati Cyanide. It was gonna be a long night at central booking.

Larry knew that night that Mavis
should never again drink eggnog.

Not even Veronica's magnificent mink could muffle the timbre of her backdoor trumpet.

Timmy suddenly understood the dangers of following through. He only wished he hadn't worn his favorite jump suit to breakfast.

Neville was confused by Fanny's unusual seduction technique. Fanny on the other hand knew her one-cheek sneak was fail-proof.

Commander Hornblower knew that if he held this one in much longer the fire might escape the hold.

'Ok. Who cooked the cauliflower cocktail?'

Frank had come over to shoot the breeze. This was not how Rita imagined being swept off her feet.

Burglary was not the only crime the
Bugle brothers committed that day.

Steve was sure he had just
ripped a seam with that one.

Clark knew that as soon as Louise started
using that fan . . . date-night was over.

Clarissa feared it might have been a wet one.

Smithers had been with the family for generations.
But his constant flatulence was starting to affect his work.

Woodward had a new suspect for the
whistle-blower . . . and it was an inside job!

The dinner party had been an unmitigated success . . .
until Mrs Guffington's cauliflower soufflé suddenly
made an unwelcome re-appearance.

Lady Winthorpe wanted Miss Clara to feel comfortable in her company, but this was ridiculous.

'Hey, thunder buns . . . a little warning would be nice!'

In that instant Elvira realised that she had never truly experienced the scent of death.

Caesar massively regretted
switching to a high fiber diet.

'I guess this is a bad time to tell you
I had cabbage surprise for lunch . . . ?'

Betsy had always loved Marcel's ruggedness,
but he'd just crossed the line . . .

Clyde was just about fed up with
Cybil's constant cushion creepers.

Neil sensed the time was right to ask
Mr Tibbs for a pay rise . . . unfortunately his
sudden and horrific foul howl really killed the mood.

Gertie was all too familiar with Crispin's special vintage release and could only pray the stench would dissipate before the eulogy!

Spencer wondered how long the others would pretend to ignore his silent-but-deadly fog slicer.

'I swear it wasn't me, baby . . .'

Published by Plexus Publishing Limited
The Studio, Hillgate Place
18-20 Balham Hill
London SW12 9ER
www.plexusbooks.com

British Library Cataloguing in Publication Data
A catalogue record for this book is available from
the British Library

ISBN-13: 978-0-85965-513-2

Printed in Great Britain by Bell & Bain Ltd, Glasgow

Acknowledgements

We would like to thank the following agencies for photographs:
Library of Congress; Getty Images/John Kobal Foundation;
Getty Images/John Kobal Foundation; Getty Images/John Kobal
Foundation; Getty Images/John Kobal Foundation; Getty Images/
John Kobal Foundation; Getty Images/John Kobal Foundation;
Getty Images/John Kobal Foundation; Getty Images/Hulton
Archive/Stringer; Getty Images/John Kobal Foundation; Getty
Images/John Kobal Foundation/Robert Coburn; Getty Images/
John Kobal Foundation; Getty Images/John Kobal Foundation;
Getty Images/John Kobal Foundation; Getty Images/John Kobal
Foundation; Getty Images/John Kobal Foundation; Getty Images/
John Kobal Foundation; Getty Images/John Kobal Foundation;
Getty Images/John Kobal Foundation; Getty Images/John Kobal
Foundation; Getty Images/John Kobal Foundation; Getty Images/
John Kobal Foundation/Florence Vandamm; Getty Images/
Margaret Chute/Stringer; Getty Images/John Kobal Foundation;
Getty Images/John Kobal Foundation; Getty Images/Silver Screen
Collection; Getty Images/John Kobal Foundation; Getty Images/
John Kobal Foundation; Getty Images/John Kobal Foundation;
Getty Images/John Kobal Foundation; Getty Images/John Kobal
Foundation; Getty Images/John Kobal Foundation; Getty Images/
John Kobal Foundation; Getty Images/John Kobal Foundation;
Getty Images/John Kobal Foundation/Clarence Sinclair Bull;
Getty Images/John Kobal Foundation; Getty Images/John Kobal
Foundation; Getty Images/John Kobal Foundation; Getty Images/
John Kobal Foundation; Getty Images/John Kobal Foundation;
Getty Images/John Kobal Foundation; Getty Images/John Kobal
Foundation; Getty Images/John Kobal Foundation.